The Trial of Christ

The Trial of Christ
by David K. Breed

Start Publishing PD LLC
Copyright © 2024 by Start Publishing PD LLC

All rights reserved, including the right to reproduce this book or portions thereof in any form whatsoever.

Start Publishing PD is a registered trademark of Start Publishing PD LLC
Manufactured in the United States of America

Cover art: Shutterstock/Taisiya Kozorez

Cover design: Jennifer Do

10 9 8 7 6 5 4 3 2 1

ISBN 979-8-8809-2204-8

FOREWORD

By Reverend Clarence Edward Macartney
Pastor, First Presbyterian Church
Pittsburgh, Pa.

The great fact, and the Eternal Fact, in the life of Jesus was his death for our sins upon the Cross. This was the fact which St. Paul declared he preached to the Corinthians "first of all"; not that they were the first to hear it; not that it merely came first in the enumeration of the great truths of the Gospel; but that it was first in importance, the Eternal Fact of Redemption. The steps, therefore, by which Jesus was brought to the Cross, although ever of the greatest interest, are secondary in importance to the death of Christ on the Cross.

Christian lawyers have always found the records of the trial of Jesus of great interest. This interest has led the author of this book to make a careful study from a lawyer's standpoint of the trial of Jesus. He brings out the fact that Jesus was tried six times in twelve hours; before Annas, before Caiaphas, before the Sanhedrin, before Pilate, before Herod, before Pilate again. Of course, the real judicial trial was that before the Sanhedrin. According to the author there were seventeen errors in these trials which might be classified as "reversible;" that is, such errors as today would warrant a superior court in reversing the judgment of the lower court. Among these errors he notes the following: No process could take place on one of the feast days; no process could be started at night. Caiaphas publicly declared before the trial that Christ deserved death. Jesus had no counsel to defend him. Pilate declared Jesus not guilty, and yet accepted the verdict of the mob and sent him to crucifixion. It was illegal for the Sanhedrin to convict a man on the same day as the trial.

This is a carefully done book, and those who wish to follow out the experiences of our Lord on that same night in which he was betrayed will find much of interest and instruction in it.

Unlike some others who have written about the trial of Jesus, this author has a true and scriptural understanding of what the trial of Jesus led to; that is, his sacrificial and atoning death for sin upon the Cross; for he says,

"Christianity is not a religion; it is a revelation. The word 'religion' comes from a Greek root meaning the act of man searching out for God, pagan man trying to find God. But when Very God became flesh and dwelt among us, revealed Himself in the person of Christ, and died to save us from our sin, religion ceased for all believers in Jesus."

Those who read this book may be interested to know that the author, a St. Louis lawyer, comes naturally by an interest in theological and scriptural questions, for he is a direct descendant of America's greatest thinker and theologian, Jonathan Edwards.

Clarence Edward Macartney.

TABLE OF CONTENTS

FOREWORD.	5
THE SCOPE OF OUR STUDY.	8
LEGAL BACKGROUND AND SOURCES OF THE RECORD.	10
THE RECORD OF THE TRIALS.	13
REVERSIBLE ERRORS.	25
FIVE COURTS AND SIX TRIALS.	28
ARGUMENT AS TO JEWISH TRIALS.	32
ERRORS IN THE ROMAN TRIALS.	37
A LESSON IN CITIZENSHIP.	39
EPILOGUE—OUR REDEEMER.	42
APPENDIX A—LAWYERS IN THE SANHEDRIN.	45
APPENDIX B—BIBLIOGRAPHY.	48

THE SCOPE OF OUR STUDY

"For God so loved the world, that he gave his only begotten Son, that whosoever believeth in him should not perish, but have everlasting life." The death of Christ as the sacrifice of God for man is the greatest fact in the story of salvation, except His glorious resurrection. No legalistic study of The Trial of Christ can take the place of the Evangelistic message of The Christ. To many lawyers, no trial of history is quite so interesting as the Trial of Christ. Our purpose will be to re-examine the trial in the light of the Roman and Jewish laws of that era, and our laws today, in order to call the attention of Christian people to the legal significance of that trial—and, perchance, to demonstrate again the fact that there is no substitute for Christian faith.

Our approach to the subject will be in legalistic style, a style perhaps not too familiar to lay minds, but that most adaptable to our subject.

In preparing a case on Appeal today, an attorney edits and files in The Supreme Court

(1) a digest of the charges, the pleadings, the testimony and judgment in the lower court (called collectively "The Record"),

(2) a list of the points on which he intends to rely as grounds for reversal of the judgment below (called an "Assignment of Errors"),

(3) a repetition of the Assignment of Errors, with reference to legal publications as authority for the propositions relied on as error, usually somewhat amplified in form and known as "Points and Authorities," and, finally, (4) an essay discussing the record, errors and authorities in logical sequence and known as an "Argument." In most Appellate and Supreme Courts these documents must be printed and the practice is to print The Record as a separate volume, combining the Errors, Authorities and Argument under another cover.

We will follow the above classification with one modification, that we will combine the Authorities with the Errors and give within these pages a statement of the following:

A. In Chapter II, some comment on the nature of law and the sources of the Record of The Trial of Christ;

B. In Chapter III, that Record, as we have it in the four Gospels;

C. In Chapter IV, a discussion of the term "Reversible Error" and a list of the Errors in The Trial of Christ;

D. In Chapters V, VI, VII and VIII, we explain and argue the various errors listed in Chapter IV, and draw from these arguments A Lesson in Citizenship; and,

E. In the Epilogue we summarize our study to emphasize that Christ is Our Redeemer.

A word as to the authorities. Our study is not unique, and an attempt is made to credit its sources, both legalistic and theological. For brevity's sake, the standard legal citations are given in our footnotes and the theological works referred to in an abbreviated form, to all of which a key is found in an Appendix.

LEGAL BACKGROUND AND SOURCES OF THE RECORD

To a Christian Lawyer, the Trial of Christ has a deep significance because we know that the legalistic errors in that trial, condemnable though they be, nevertheless fulfilled prophecy and thereby served a purpose. Theological writers have many works that show how the Old Testament Prophecies were fulfilled in what did take place; indeed, many passages of the Gospel Record are quoted from the Prophets. A further word on this point will be found in our Epilogue, but we limit ourselves, for the present, to the legal phases of the Trial of Christ.

In using the word "trial" in its legalistic sense, the author is not unmindful of the fact that Christ was thrice "tried", or, more properly speaking, tempted by the Devil. However, any study of the trial in the spiritual sense is left to homiletical writings, such as Dr. Clarence Edward Macartney's recent book, Trials of Great Men of the Bible, in which Chapters XI and XV deal with the temptations of Christ.

Christian and Jewish people alike in every generation are taught considerable from the Old Testament Scriptures dealing with the Mosaic Law. Those who are not themselves attorneys perhaps little realize that many of the basic principles of modern law go back to ancient roots. At least one modern writer has attempted to prove, for example, that the idea of due process of law expressed in the Fourteenth Amendment to the Constitution of The United States was not an invention of reformers of our Civil War era but rather a recognition in modern law that it is illegal to punish one who has not been duly convicted of crime upon a trial conducted with due deference to the law of evidence.

In modern times, Sir William Blackstone, a great British statesman and jurist, wrote that "When civil society is once formed, government at the same time results, of course, as necessary to preserve and to keep that society in order. Unless some superior be constituted, whose commands and decisions all the members are bound to obey, they would still remain as in a state of nature, without any judge upon earth to define their several rights and redress their several wrongs." In other words, the function of Government is to give all people security from the encroachment of one another, upon what has been called in our basic American law, "Life, Liberty and the pursuit of Happiness."

To make our point very clear, before proceeding to a further chapter where we will deal in detail with "Reversible Errors," it seems well to emphasize that in modern legal parlance a mistake made by a trial judge is deemed Reversible Error, if the mistake is so serious as to be grounds for a new trial. Glaring examples would be to let a man's partner sit on a jury at his trial; for a Judge to hear a case in which lie is an interested party, or has already formed an opinion; or to permit a witness to testify to hearsay instead of facts. These are some of the "Reversible Errors" on which a new trial can be had and are often spoken of by misinformed business men as "technicalities," as when they say a certain gangster "got off on a technicality" or "got a new trial on a technicality."

Before leaving our discussion of legal principles, it seems well to point out that after a Court Reporter has taken down the testimony of a trial in the first instance, upon appeal being taken to a higher court by either party, the higher Court does not again hear the witnesses but passes upon the case upon the typewritten or printed transcription of the notes taken by the Court Reporter. Such notes together with the various formal documents filed by lawyers in the lower court are (as we have written) referred to collectively as "the record on appeal." Although the Court erred in the Trial of Christ by not keeping any records (so far as we know) when at that time court reporters were known to Roman and Hebrew law and custom, 4 the record in the synoptic Gospels is, however, sufficient to enable us to pass intelligent review, were we an Appellate Court, upon the illegalities of the Trial of Christ.

THE RECORD OF THE TRIALS

We have referred in a previous Chapter to the fact that the Gospels refer in some detail to the Trial of Christ. Since we have referred to the record on appeal as the legal basis for trial study, no record of an actual court-reporter being extant, we include as the best record available the passages given us in the Gospels. Those passages, containing a record of The Trial of Christ are:

Matthew 26:57-27:2; 27:11-26;
Mark 14:53-15:15;
Luke 22:54-23:24; and,
John 18:12-19:16; inclusive.

We quote the record, as given in the Authorized Version:

ST. MATTHEW, in Chapters 26 and 27, verses as numbered:
Chapter 26 of Matthew:
"57. And they that had laid hold on Jesus led him away to Caiaphas the high priest, where the scribes and elders were assembled.

58. But Peter followed him afar off unto the high priest's palace, and went in, and sat with the servants, to see the end.

59. Now the chief priests, and elders, and all the council, sought false witness against Jesus, to put him to death;

60. But found none: yea, though many false witnesses came, yet found they none. At the last came two false witnesses,

61. And said, This fellow said, I am able to destroy the temple of God, and to build it in three days.

62. And the high priest arose, and said unto him, Answerest thou nothing? what is it which these witness against thee?

63. But Jesus held his peace. And the high priest answered and said unto him, I adjure thee by the living God, that thou tell us whether thou be the Christ, the Son of God.

64. Jesus saith unto him, Thou hast said: nevertheless I say unto you, Hereafter shall ye see the Son of man sitting on the right hand of power, and coming in the clouds of heaven.

65. Then the high priest rent his clothes, saying, He hath spoken blasphemy; what further need have we of witnesses? behold, now ye have heard his blasphemy.

66. What think ye? They answered and said, He is guilty of death.

67. Then did they spit in his face, and buffeted him; and others smote him with the palms of their hands,

68. Saying, Prophesy unto us, thou Christ, Who is he that smote thee?

69. Now Peter sat without in the palace: and a damsel came unto him, saying, Thou also wast with Jesus of Galilee.

70. But he denied before them all, saying, I know not what thou sayest.

71. And when he was gone out into the porch, another maid saw him, and said unto them that were there, This fellow was also with Jesus of Nazareth.

72. And again he denied with an oath, I do not know the man.

73. And after a while came unto him they that stood by, and said to Peter, Surely thou also art one of them; for thy speech bewrayeth thee.

74. Then began he to curse and to swear, saying, I know not the man. And immediately the cock crew.

75. And Peter remembered the word of Jesus, which said unto him, Before the cock crow, thou shalt deny me thrice. And he went out, and wept bitterly."

Chapter 27 of Matthew:

"When the morning was come, all the chief priests and elders of the people took counsel against Jesus to put him to death;

2. And when they had bound him, they led him away, and delivered him to Pontius Pilate the governor."

"11. And Jesus stood before the governor: and the governor asked him, saying, Art thou the King of the Jews? And Jesus said unto him, Thou sayest.

12. And when he was accused of the chief priests and elders, he answered nothing.

13. Then said Pilate unto him, Hearest thou not how many things they witness against thee?

14. And he answered him to never a word; insomuch that the governor marvelled greatly.

15. Now at that feast the governor was wont to release unto the people a prisoner, whom they would.

16. And they had then a notable prisoner, called Barabbas.

17. Therefore when they were gathered together, Pilate said unto them, Whom will ye that I release unto you? Barabbas, or Jesus which is called Christ?

18. For he knew that for envy they had delivered him.

19. When he was set down on the judgment seat, his wife sent unto him, saying, Have thou nothing to do with that just man: for I have suffered many things this day in a dream because of him.

20. But the chief priests and elders persuaded the multitude that they should ask Barabbas, and destroy Jesus.

21. The governor answered and said unto them, Whether of the twain will ye that I release unto you? They said, Barabbas.

22. Pilate saith unto them, What shall I do then with Jesus which is called Christ? They all say unto him, Let him be crucified.

23. And the governor said, Why, what evil hath he done? But they cried out the more, saying, Let him be crucified.

24. When Pilate saw that he could prevail nothing, but that rather a tumult was made, he took water, and washed his hands before the multitude, saying, I am innocent of the blood of this just person: see ye to it.

25. Then answered all the people, and said, His blood be on us, and on our children.

26. Then released he Barabbas unto them; and when he had scourged Jesus, he delivered him to be crucified."

ST. MARK, in Chapters 14 and 15, verses as numbered:
Chapter 14 of Mark:

"53. And they led Jesus away to the high priest: and with him were assembled all the chief priests and the elders and the scribes.

54. And Peter followed him afar off, even into the palace of the high priest: and he sat with the servants, and warmed himself at the fire.

55. And the chief priests and all the council sought for witness against Jesus to put him to death; and f ouiid none.

56. For many bare false witness against him, but their witness 6 agreed not together.

57. And there arose certain, and bare false witness against him, saying,

58. We heard him say, I will destroy this temple that is made with hands, and within three days I will build another made without hands.

59. But neither so did their witness agree together.

60. And the high priest stood up in the midst, and asked Jesus, saying, Answerest thou nothing? what is it which these witness against thee?

61. But he held his peace, and answered nothing. Again the high priest asked him, and said unto him, Art thou the Christ, the Son of the Blessed?

62. And Jesus said, I am: and ye shall see the Son of man sitting on the right hand of power, and coming in the clouds of heaven.

63. Then the high priest rent his clothes, and saith, What need we any further witnesses?

64. Ye have heard the blasphemy: what think ye? And they all condemned him to be guilty of death.

65. And some began to spit on him, and to cover his face, and to buffet him, and to say unto him, Prophesy: and the servants did strike him with the palms of their hands.

66. And as Peter was beneath in the palace, there cometh one of the maids of the high priest:

67. And when she saw Peter warming himself, she looked upon

The Trial of Christ

him, and said, And thou also wast with Jesus of Nazareth.

68. But he denied, saying, I know not, neither understand I what thou sayest. And he went out into the porch; and the cock crew.

69. And a maid saw him again, and began to say to them that stood by, This is one of them.

70. And he denied it again. And a little after, they that stood by said again to Peter, Surely thou art one of them: for thou art a Galilean, and thy speech agreeth thereto.

71. But he began to curse and to swear, saying, I know not this man of whom ye speak.

72. And the second time the cock crew. And Peter called to mind the word that Jesus said unto him, Before the cock crow twice, thou shalt deny me thrice. And when he thought thereon, he wept."

Chapter 15 of Mark:

"And straightway in the morning the chief priests held a consultation with the elders and scribes and the whole council, and bound Jesus, and carried him away, and delivered him to Pilate.

2. And Pilate asked him, Art thou the King of the Jews? And he answering said unto him, Thou sayest it.

3. And the chief priests accused him of many things: but he answered nothing.

4. And Pilate asked him again, saying, Answerest thou nothing? behold how many things they witness against thee.

5. But Jesus yet answered nothing; so that Pilate marvelled.

6. Now at that feast he released unto them one prisoner, whomsoever they desired.

7. And there was one named Barabbas, which lay bound with them that had made insurrection with him, who had committed murder in the insurrection.

8. And the multitude crying aloud began to desire him to do as he had ever done unto them.

9. But Pilate answered them, saying, Will ye that I release unto you the King of the Jews?

10. For he knew that the chief priests had delivered him for envy.

11. But the chief priests moved the people, that he should rather release Barabbas unto them.

12. And Pilate answered and said again unto them, What will ye then that I shall do unto him whom ye call the King of the Jews?

13. And they cried out again, Crucify him.

14. Then Pilate said unto them, Why, what evil hath he done? And they cried out the more exceedingly, Crucify him.

15. And so Pilate, willing to content the people, released Barabbas unto them, and delivered Jesus, when he had scourged him, to be crucified."

ST. LUKE, in Chapters 22 and 23, verses as numbered:
Chapter 22 of Luke:
"54. Then took they him, and led him, and brought him into the high priest's house. And Peter followed afar off.

55. And when they had kindled a fire in the midst of the hall, and were set down together, Peter sat down among them.

56. But a certain maid beheld him as he sat by the fire, and earnestly looked upon him, and said, This man was also with him.

57. And he denied him, saying, Woman, I know him not.

58. And after a little while another saw him, and said, Thou art also of them. And Peter said, Man, I am not.

59. And about the space of one hour after another confidently affirmed, saying, Of a truth this fellow also was with him: for he is a Galilean.

60. And Peter said, Man, I know not what thou sayest. And immediately, while he yet spake, the cock crew.

61. And the Lord turned, and looked upon Peter. And Peter remembered the word of the Lord, how he had said unto him, Before the cock crow, thou shalt deny me thrice.

62. And Peter went out, and wept bitterly.

63. And the men that held Jesus mocked him, and smote him.

64. And when they had blindfolded him, they struck him on the face, and asked him, saying, Prophesy, who is it that smote thee?

65. And many other things blasphemously spake they against

him.

66. And as soon as it was day, the elders of the people and the chief priests and the scribes came together, and led him into their council, saying,

67. Art thou the Christ? tell us. And he said unto them, If I tell you, ye will not believe:

68. And if I also ask you, ye will not answer me, nor let me go.

69. Hereafter shall the Son of man sit on the right hand of the power of God.

70. Then said they all, Art thou then the Son of God? And he said unto them, Ye say that I am.

71. And they said, What need we any further witness? for we ourselves have heard of his own mouth."

Chapter 23 of Luke:
"And the whole multitude of them arose, and led him unto Pilate.

2. And they began to accuse him, saying, We found this fellow perverting the nation, and forbidding to give tribute to Caesar, saying, that he himself is Christ a King.

3. And Pilate asked him, saying, Art thou the King of the Jews? And he answered him and said, Thou sayest it.

4. Then said Pilate to the chief priests and to the people, I find no fault in this man.

5. And they were the more fierce, saying, He stirreth up the people, teaching throughout all Jewry, beginning from Galilee to this place.

6. When Pilate heard of Galilee, he asked whether the man were a Galilean.

7. And as soon as he knew that he belonged unto Herod's jurisdiction, he sent him to Herod, who himself also was at Jerusalem at that time.

8. And when Herod saw Jesus, he was exceeding glad: for he was desirous to see him of a long season, because he had heard many things of him; and he hoped to have seen some miracle done by him.

9. Then he questioned with him in many words; but he answered him nothing.

10. And the chief priests and scribes stood and vehemently accused him.

11. And Herod with his men of war set him at nought, and mocked him, and arrayed him in a gorgeous robe, and sent him again to Pilate.

12. And the same day Pilate and Herod were made friends together: for before they were at enmity between themselves.

13. And Pilate, when he had called together the chief priests and the rulers and the people,

14. Said unto them, Ye have brought this man unto me, as one that perverteth the people: and, behold, I, having examined him before you, have found no fault in this man touching those things whereof ye accuse him:

15. No, nor yet Herod: for I sent you to him; and, lo, nothing worthy of death is done unto him.

16. I will therefore chastise him, and release him.

17. (For of necessity he must release one unto them at the feast.)

18. And they cried out all at once, saying, Away with this man, and release unto us Barabbas:

19. (Who for a certain sedition made in the city, and for murder, was cast into prison.)

20. Pilate therefore, willing to release Jesus, spake again to them.

21. But they cried, saying, Crucify him, crucify him.

22. And he said unto them the third time, Why, what evil hath he done? I have found no cause of death in him: I will therefore chastise him, and let him go.

23. And they were instant with loud voices, requiring that he might be crucified. And the voices of them and of the chief priests prevailed.

24. And Pilate gave sentence that it should be as they required."

ST. JOHN, in Chapters 18 and 19, verses as numbered:

Chapter 18 of John:

"12. Then the band and the captain and officers of the Jews took Jesus, and bound him,

13. And led him away to Annas first; for he was father in law to Caiaphas, which was the high priest that same year.

14. Now Caiaphas was he, which gave counsel to the Jews, that it was expedient that one man should die for the people.

15. And Simon Peter followed Jesus, and so did another disciple: that disciple was known unto the high priest, and went in with Jesus into the palace of the high priest.

16. But Peter stood at the door without. Then went out that other disciple, which was known unto the high priest, and spake unto her that kept the door, and brought in Peter.

17. Then saith the damsel that kept the door unto Peter, Art not thou also one of this man's disciples? He saith, I am not.

18. And the servants and officers stood there, who had made a fire of coals; for it was cold: and they warmed themselves: and Peter stood with them, and warmed himself.

19. The high priest then asked Jesus of his disciples, and of his doctrine.

20. Jesus answered him, I spake openly to the world; I ever taught in the synagogue, and in the temple, whither the Jews always resort; and in secret have I said nothing.

21. Why askest thou me? ask them which heard me, what I have said unto them: behold, they know what I said.

22. And when he had thus spoken, one of the officers which stood by struck Jesus with the palm of his hand, saying, Answerest thou the high priest so?

23. Jesus answered him, If I have spoken evil, bear witness of the evil: but if well, why smitest thou me?

24. Now Annas had sent him bound unto Caiaphas the high priest.

25. And Simon Peter stood and warmed himself. They said therefore unto him, Art not thou also one of his disciples? He denied it, and said, I am not.

26. One of the servants of the high priest, being his kinsman

whose ear Peter cut off, saith, Did not I see thee in the garden with him?

27. Peter then denied again: and immediately the cock crew.

28. Then led they Jesus from Caiaphas unto the hall of judgment: and it was early; and they themselves went not into the judgment hall, lest they should be defiled; but that they might eat the passover.

29. Pilate then went out unto them, and said, What accusation bring ye against this man?

30. They answered and said unto him, If he were not a malefactor, we would not have delivered him up unto thee.

31. Then said Pilate unto them, Take ye him, and judge him according to your law. The Jews therefore said unto him, it is not lawful for us to put any man to death:

32. That the saying of Jesus might be fulfilled, which he spake, signifying what death he should die.

33. Then Pilate entered into the judgment hall again, and called Jesus, and said unto him, Art thou the King of the Jews?

34. Jesus answered him, Sayest thou this thing of thyself, or did others tell it thee of me?

35. Pilate answered, Am I a Jew? Thine own nation and the chief priests have delivered thee unto me: what hast thou done?

36. Jesus answered, My kingdom is not of this world: if my kingdom were of this world, then would my servants fight, that I should not be delivered to the Jews: but now is my kingdom not from hence.

37. Pilate therefore said unto him, Art thou a king then? Jesus answered, Thou sayest that I am a king. To this end was I born, and for this cause came I into the world, that I should bear witness unto the truth. Every one that is of the truth heareth my voice.

38. Pilate saith unto him, What is truth? And when he had said this, he went out again unto the Jews, and saith unto them, I find in him no fault at all.

39. But ye have a custom, that I should release unto you one at the passover: will ye therefore that I release unto you the King of the Jews?

40. Then cried they all again, saying, Not this man, but Barabbas. Now Barabbas was a robber."

Chapter 19 of John:

"Then Pilate therefore took Jesus, and scourged him.

2. And the soldiers platted a crown of thorns, and put it on his head, and they put on him a purple robe,

3. And said, Hail, King of the Jews! and they smote him with their hands.

4. Pilate therefore went forth again, and saith unto them, Behold, I bring him forth to you, that ye may know that I find no fault in him.

5. Then came Jesus forth, wearing the crown of thorns, and the purple robe. And Pilate saith unto them, Behold the man!

6. When the chief priests therefore and officers saw him, they cried out, saying, Crucify him, crucify him. Pilate saith unto them, Take ye him, and crucify him: for I find no fault in him.

7. The Jews answered him, We have a law, and by our law he ought to die, because he made himself the Son of God.

8. When Pilate therefore heard that saying, he was the more afraid;

9. And went again into the judgment hall, and saith unto Jesus, Whence art thou? But Jesus gave him no answer.

10. Then saith Pilate unto him, Speakest thou not unto me? knowest thou not that I have power to crucify thee, and have power to release thee?

11. Jesus answered, Thou couldest have no power at all against me, except it were given thee from above: therefore he that delivereth me unto thee hath the greater sin.

12. And from thenceforth Pilate sought to release him: but the Jews cried out, saying, If thou let this man go, thou art not Caesar's friend: whosoever maketh himself a king speaketh against Caesar.

13. When Pilate therefore heard that saying, he brought Jesus forth, and sat down in the judgment seat in a place that is called the Pavement, but in the Hebrew, Gabbatha.

14. And it was the preparation of the passover, and about the

sixth hour: and he saith unto the Jews, Behold your King!

15. But they cried out, Away with him, away with him, crucify him. Pilate saith unto them, Shall I crucify your King? The chief priests answered, We have no king but Caesar.

16. Then delivered he him therefore unto them to be crucified. And they took Jesus, and led him away."

REVERSIBLE ERRORS

"Reversible Error" is defined in modern law as "such an error as warrants the appellate court in reversing the judgment and remanding the cause." For generations an error has been held not reversible unless, at the time it was made, the party against whom it was made, through his attorney, made specific objection to the action of the trial court and saved a specific "exception" to the ruling; but in 1943 Missouri abolished exceptions and provided in its new Code for Civil Procedure that "it is sufficient that a party, at the time the ruling of the Court is made or sought, makes known to the court the action which he desires the court to take or his objection to the action of the court and his grounds therefor; and if a party has no opportunity to object to a ruling or order at the time it is made, the absence of an objection does not thereafter prejudice him." The said Code, Section 140, goes on to say that "No Appellate court shall reverse any judgment, unless it believes that error was committed by the trial court against appellant, and materially affecting the merits of the action." Exceptions still have to be saved in criminal causes in Missouri, and from a purely technical standpoint there may have been no reversible error in the Trial of Christ, merely because Jesus saved no exceptions, made no objection,—"opened not his mouth." The only statements Jesus did make were in the nature of admissions of His power.

IF, however, errors had been pointed out to the trial courts—Annas, Caiaphas, The Sanhedrin, Pilate and Herod—then IF an appeal had been had, Jesus would have been able to assign seventeen errors in the trials. We shall note these errors here and annotate them in the footnotes, before passing on to discuss the trials in detail.

These errors are:

1. No process could take place on the Jewish Sabbath or on feast days.

2. No process could be started at night or even afternoon for a trial before a regular Sanhedrin court.

3. It was error for Caiaphas, acting as Judge, to have sought words from the mouth of Christ upon which to convict Him, without first making a prima-facie case with other witnesses.

4. Caiaphas' Palace was not the meeting place of the Sanhedrin: it was error to hold a trial there.

5. It was error for Caiaphas to have acted as Judge after having publicly declared that Christ deserved death.

6. It was error to have left Him unguarded, to the unrestrained license of the mob in the gallery of Caiaphas' palace or court for an hour or more.

7. The Sanhedrin had no jurisdiction in Capital Cases, having been divested of that jurisdiction by the Romans forty years before.

8. The Sanhedrin, if existent, had no power except at a regular meeting.

9. It was error not to appoint someone to defend Him—Jesus had no counsel.

10. It was error not to have "warned" the witnesses in this capital case, in a Sanhedrin court.

11. The courts erred by not taking into consideration the guilt or innocence of Jesus.

12. It was error to take Christ, as prisoner, before Annas.

13. In modern times it would have been error to require Christ to testify y as a witness against Himself, but in those days in a trial for Blasphemy there seems to have been authority in favor of requiring what we know as "self incrimination" —this will be discussed in detail in a later chapter.

14. Roman Law required trials to be public, and the private trial of Christ before Annas and Caiaphas was error.

15. It was error to convict a man on the testimony of false witnesses;—under modern law the Jury determines the credibility of the Witnesses.

16. Pilate having announced Jesus not guilty, erred in permitting the verdict of the "mob" to stand. The record shows Christ, after Pilate found "no harm" in Him, was sent to Herod, then back to Pilate, then turned over to be crucified.

17. It was unlawful and therefore error for the Sanhedrin to convict on the same day as the trial; they could acquit the same day but had to hold a verdict of "guilty" under advisement at least two days.

FIVE COURTS AND SIX TRIALS

Jesus, arrested about midnight in the Garden of Gethsemane, was tried six times before he was crucified the following noon. Six trials in twelve hours! Peloubet's Bible Dictionary gives the time of this chronology as follows:

1.	Before Annas	FRIDAY
2.	Before Caiaphas	1 to 5 A. M.
3.	Before the Sanhedrin	
4.	Before Pilate	5 to 6 A. M.
5.	Before Herod	
6.	Before Pilate Again	

From a standpoint of technical law, the personnel of a legally constituted court is of slight significance. Yet historians know that the course of law has been at times altered and history influenced by the character of judges. Marshall and Holmes, of the United States Supreme Court, Lord Mansfield, Lord Eldon, and Sir William Blackstone of England, Moses of the Hebrews, Justinian of the Romans, Solon of the Greeks, Dean Wigmore of Northwestern University Law School and Dean Pound of Harvard have all made great contributions to law and legal literature. So, in a study of the trial of Christ, one should know something about Annas, Caiaphas, Pilate, and Herod.

The Trial of Christ

This is particularly true because, as we shall see, Christian and Jewish scholars alike agree that the trial of Christ was not a proper trial, the Christians contending that prophecy was fulfilled, the Jews contending that the Christians falsely blame the Jews for a Roman crime.

A. BIOGRAPHICAL

Annas, his five sons, and his father-in-law Caiaphas, all held the Jewish High-Priesthood during the first century, A. D., and it appears from the New Testament that at the time of the arrest of Jesus, Caiaphas was actually in office as High Priest, his son-in-law, Annas, being a former High Priest but also holding the title for life. Caiaphas was a wily politician in the Sanhedrin who had held office as High Priest for eighteen years, although custom was to elect for a one year term. Rollins describes Annas as a nefarious moneylending Sadducee, a political friend of the Romans, while we know that Caiaphas had conspired with Judas to betray Christ; and that none of the writers give either man any praise.

Herod was Roman Governor of Galilee; Pilate, of Judea. Both happened to be in Jerusalem for the Passover crowd. Herod was a son of Herod the Great, who had ordered the slaughter of the infants thirty years before, and probably hated Jesus.

Pilate was the fifth Roman governor of Judea 45 and was noted for his cruel and arbitrary administration of the government. He was also weak at times and has been greatly criticized by historians. Rabbi Drucker, in his analysis of the Trial of Christ, not only pictures Pilate as a persecutor of the Jews but states that Caiaphas was a Roman spy and that the historian Tacitus correctly stated that "Jesus, called Christ, was crucified by Pilate for promoting a rebellion among the Jews." We do know that Pilate was a craven coward and was afraid to release Jesus.

B. CHRONOLOGY OF THE TRIALS

1. Jesus was taken first to Annas, who was not then High Priest and had no power, so took no formal action but merely "marked time" as it were, until Caiaphas and the Sanhedrin were ready for

action.

2. Caiaphas was High Priest and seems to have questioned Jesus privately prior to the convening of the Sanhedrin. Mr. Chandler, in his two volume work on the Trial of Jesus devotes a whole volume to the Biblical Record, Jewish Law and the Jewish Trials (Volume I), filling up his second volume with a discussion of the Roman Trial of Jesus, and while most of his discussion is interesting, it is longer than necessary. Suffice it to say that Caiaphas' examination of Jesus was merely preparatory to the formal Sanhedrin trial. John gives the clearest account of the action before Caiaphas alone, probably in the presence only of Peter who had followed afar off.

3. The Sanhedrin was a court in the limited sense of the word. It had legislative, executive, judicial, civil, criminal, and ecclesiastical powers over the Jews, and its judges were 72 descendants of Moses. It had to meet legally in daylight, in the forenoon, in a certain room, with court reporters present; and its rules of procedure were so strict that an unanimous verdict of guilt meant acquittal. There could be unanimous verdicts of acquittal, but no unanimous verdicts of guilt. But the Sanhedrin (in violation of its rules) moved quickly to try Jesus on a charge of Blasphemy, on the testimony of two false witnesses who contradicted each other, but Jesus here broke His silence and said He is Christ. Then the Sanhedrin unanimously found Him guilty of Blasphemy, but had no power to put Him to death without the consent of Pilate. The Sanhedrists at this point spit on Jesus, while some struck Him with their hands. In the morning, they sent Jesus to Pilate.

4. Pilate was Roman Governor and not interested at all in the Jewish charges of Blasphemy, so he found no harm in Jesus. He was impressed though with the "trumped up" charge of Treason; but when Jesus said His kingdom is "not of this world," and that Pilate had "no power at all against me except it were given thee from above: therefore he that hath delivered me unto thee hath the greater sin," Pilate was less interested than before and sent Jesus to Herod.

The Trial of Christ

5. Herod questioned Jesus at length but, getting no answer, sent Jesus back to Pilate.

6. Pilate had Jesus before him a second time, and again tried to appease the Jews by releasing Jesus as a Holiday Pardon, but they demanded the release of Barabbas, then Pilate delivered Jesus up to be crucified by Roman soldiers on the demand of the Jewish mob. However, Pilate required that it be inscribed over the Cross, "Jesus of Nazareth the King of the Jews. "

ARGUMENT AS TO JEWISH TRIALS

We have listed in a previous chapter some seventeen reversible errors in the trial of Christ. Chandler, in his lengthy discussion, lists many more. Rollins lists eighteen. But the number is not important because one error is enough to justify reversal of a case under modern law, and there have been instances where many allegations of error were brushed aside by an appellate court, as in the Lindbergh kidnapping case, where Mr. Hauptmann unsuccessfully charged the Court with 57 errors. Men like Rabbi Drucker, in examining the Trial of Christ, claim it never could have taken place because the members of the Sanhedrin were too learned to err as widely as they did, and too religious to hold such proceedings before the morning hour of worship in the Temple. But ample proof of what was done exists in the sacred writings of Matthew, Mark, Luke, and John, the historical writings, and the admissions of later Jewish scholars like Rabbi Klausner, to whom we have referred.

As to the particular errors in the trial, we know that the Romans had shorn the Sanhedrin of much of its old power as the highest court of Judaism; yet we also know that it was tolerated by the Romans as a sort of provisional or local government in Jerusalem at the time, much as our Government gives a partial freedom to our American Indians in tribal matters, or as the British heretofore permitted sovereignty of some Princes and Maharajahs in interior India. We do know that the Sanhedrin still had some power, subject to Appeal to the Romans; and that in modern times there has always been a like appeal from India and The Dominions to the Privy Council in England, and is now a right of appeal to The Supreme Court of the United States from colonial courts in Hawaii or Porto Rico.

Thus established, the Sanhedrin did have jurisdiction to give punishment for Blasphemy, provided it met in a certain place, during the morning hour after the morning worship service in the Temple had ended, and conducted its sessions according to all the required procedure which included rules that it should not meet on feast days or the Sabbath, nor without having court reporters present, and then should reach a verdict of guilty only on a divided vote after two days' deliberation. We have given these requirements and referred to the authorities in our chapter on the Assignments of Error.

Similar restrictions on the power of the Courts are in effect today. Title 28 of the Judicial Code of the United States covers a few hundred printed pages that are filled with the jurisdictional details of our courts—how that they shall meet in certain cities on certain days and that appeals from District Courts in the various states are heard by a particular Circuit Court of Appeals for that Circuit (or area), how the nation is divided into ten judicial circuits, how that appeals from Alaska, Hawaii, and the United States District Court for China go to the Ninth Circuit Court of Appeals (which includes the seven most western states), while those from Porto Rico go to the First Circuit (Maine Area), Virgin Islands to the Third Circuit (Pennsylvania area), and Canal Zone cases to the Fifth Circuit which embraces several states that border on the Gulf of Mexico. All ten of the Circuit Courts of Appeals are reversible on certain points by our Supreme Court.

The first two errors we assign, as to process on a Holiday, or at night, are ideas that existed from time immemorial, and still exist with modifications. No process issues in Missouri on Sundays or Holidays, for example, except where necessary to keep a defrauder or nonresident from absconding. Modern Courts can, however, validly be in session at night, although the practice is not to begin a hearing later than midafternoon, except for the convenience of some out-of-town witness who must needs go home on a night train.

The third alleged error revolves around the action of Caiaphas in trying to get Jesus to testify against himself. We all know that in modern jurisprudence, no human right is quite so closely guarded as that, in a trial before a jury no man shall be compelled to be a witness against himself in a criminal case. On the other hand, prior to the actual trial, police of our time interrogate suspects for hours in an effort to obtain a "confession", and unless unfairness or duress is shown these confessions are competent evidence. Furthermore, some scholars argue that Caiaphas' action was necessary because any witness who testified to Christ's claims of Messiahship would himself commit blasphemy. Perhaps this point may be well taken. However we feel that Jews could have been found to testify to the fact of blasphemy without repeating the exact words of our Saviour. We know that in actual courtroom practice today, witnesses frequently use the expression "obscene and vulgar language" and Judges seldom press them for exact phraseology. Our feeling is that Caiaphas went too far and that a modern Court would reverse the judgment on this point.

The fourth error we assign is that Caiaphas had no jurisdiction because his palace was not the meeting place of the Sanhedrin. English Courts at one period of their history were rather strict about the Courts at Westminster Hall. American State Courts have been more liberal, perhaps due to the fact that in pioneer days circuit judges actually rode the circuit and held court on horseback or under a tree or wherever justice demanded, although our Federal Courts have usually been better housed, more dignified, and therefore more strict in matters of place —or "venue" as we call it. In the last decade or more, however, the increase of copyright causes in our Federal Courts has caused our Judges, on occasion, to adjourn from the Courthouse to the Cinema' to determine whether or not two motion pictures were so similar as that the latter infringed the copyright of the older; and our feeling is that this point is not so important, although Edersheim points out that it would have been a valid objection at the time.

Caiaphas is alleged to have erred a fifth time, by sitting as

The Trial of Christ 35

Judge in the case after having expressed a desire for Jesus' death. No doubt there should have been several judges in the Sanhedrin trial and if any were prejudiced against Jesus, he should not sit in judgment in the case. Surely this would have been gross error before any American court today. In fact, Judges often disqualify themselves if there is any question of self-interest involved. During the third week of May, 1947, a Judge in an Illinois murder case refused to proceed and called in a substitute Judge because two sons of the regular judge were attorneys opposing each other in the case. Those who argue that Caiaphas did err in this regard base their argument on John 11:50 where Caiaphas is quoted as desiring Jesus' death, while others say there is little or no evidence as to whom Judas conspired with. We feel that error was committed.

Jesus was left unguarded on Caiaphas' Palace Porch and was abused by the mob. This was cruel and unjustified. Those who abused Him should have been punished—but as grounds of reversible error the argument is a weak one.

No modern law references can be given on several of the points, for the reason that the Courts in America have never had occasion to pass upon the powers of the Sanhedrin. As to the power of that body in Capital Cases and when not regularly in session enough has already been said.

Jesus had no counsel! Here is implied what is probably the most serious defect in the whole procedures, both Jewish and Roman. Here is a question on which there can be little doubt. All the writers agree that Jesus had no counsel, and there is no Scripture that says he did. The problem raised is as to whether there were lawyers before the Sanhedrin in those days. The writings of St. Paul abound in legal references, and there is some evidence that he was a lawyer. Chandler denies that there were counsel for Christ before the Sanhedrin, or counsel at all, ever, but says part of the Judges should have defended Him and that an unanimous verdict was error because there always had to be a doubt of guilt and if a verdict was unanimous a prisoner had to be freed. Defendants today have a constitutional right to counsel and we feel that failure to provide counsel for Jesus was error both before the Sanhedrin and, as we shall see later, before Pilate.

To summarize here: The Jewish trial was illegal from start to finish under the then existing Hebrew Law; the arrest was illegal; 83 the private examination before Caiaphas was illegal; 84 the informal indictment was illegal because the Sanhedrin was a trial court with no power to originate charges; the Sanhedrin had no power to hold a trial at night, or before the morning sacrifice or on a holiday or Sabbath; or to conclude a trial by a verdict of "guilty" on the day the trial commenced; or to convict upon an unsupported confession without corroborative evidence; or by an unanimous verdict; and sentence was passed in the wrong room, upon irregular balloting and the High Priest unlawfully rent his clothing; sentence was passed by a prejudiced court without a diligent inquiry into the merits of the case.

We submit that this last point is the crux of the case: that if the Sanhedrin had really heard and honestly weighed the evidence they would have concluded that Christ is the Messiah—is Our Redeemer!

ERRORS IN THE ROMAN TRIALS

Mr. Rollins says Rome had "nothing to do with the arrest of Christ other than to furnish the soldiers to accompany the accusers" and then goes on in a homiletical style, to review the public career of Jesus as a background for the trial, and after a brief discussion of the Sanhedrists and their actions, devotes the remainder of his book to a discussion of Pilate, Herod and Pilate's wife, in narrative fashion and without citation of authorities. Mr. Chandler devotes considerable space to extraneous discussions of Roman Law and Procedure and concludes that while Pilate commenced the hearings in proper dignity and reached an opinion that would result in an acquittal, he vacillated into compliance with the wishes of the Jewish mob. We confine ourselves to technicality as to the issues involved, and refer the reader to Chandler for a more abstract discussion of Roman Jurisprudence.

There are two documents in ancient Roman Law that are basic, The Laws of The Twelve Tables and the Code of Justinian. We need concern ourselves only with the former to convict Pilate of legal error in his treatment of Jesus. We will cite table and sentence from the Twelve Tables as we have cited Chapter and Verse from The Bible.

The Gospels give the Roman trial considerable mention, and yet only a few statements are made which we need examine in order to establish that Roman government was supreme over the Sanhedrists and that Christ "was condemned to death in the reign of Tiberius by the Procurator Pontius Pilate."

Now—What does the record show and wherein did Pilate err?

1. Pilate did not hold hearing until dawn, but some say he should have compelled the Sanhedrin to obey the Jewish and Roman law against night trials.

2. Pilate erred in permitting the Sanhedrists to examine Jesus in private when trials had to be public in those days as now.

3. Pilate erred in not requiring the testimony of witnesses, Roman Law agreeing with the Jewish and our law on this point.

4. Pilate should have released Jesus when he found "no harm" in Him. On this point the Law of the Twelve Tables is crystal clear. Archeologists have not found all of the stone fragments of The Twelve Tables, but Professor Conant explains that all have been collated by Bruns from other sources and Conant translates as Table IX, verse 6, "The decrees of the Twelve Tables forbid any uncondemned man whomever be put to death." All of the best writers agree that Pilate, finding no harm in Jesus, should have released him then and there.

A LESSON IN CITIZENSHIP

The Author has spoken before meetings of various ward organizations in St. Louis on the subject, "Political Lessons from the Trial of Christ." Under such circumstances the utmost care is taken to avoid religious differences and to point out that the trial of Christ has a three-fold significance: the Technical aspect, the Citizenship aspect, and the Messianic aspect. To an unlearned political audience the technical portion which we have reviewed has to be stated in simple terms, in order to put the larger emphasis on the idea that the remedy for legal laxity is to honestly endeavor to get reform.

To illustrate, when the Lindbergh defendant, Hauptmann, assigned in an Appellate Court some 57 alleged errors in his trial for the kidnapping and murder of young Lindbergh, a good church friend of mine ventured the opinion that he would "get off on a technicality." We are glad he did not. At the time, I told my friend that the technicalities of the law are for the protection of all people, innocent and guilty alike. The duty of a good citizen is not to wail over apparent technical miscarriages of justice but rather to join hands with his fellows to correct the existing procedural evils. How many of those who condemned the Supreme Court for avoiding a Child Labor law some twenty-five years ago, ever turned their hands to aid in the campaign to amend the Constitution of The United States so as to permit regulation of this evil? How many of those who scorn politics as "dirty" ever do anything to clean them up? How many so-called professing Christians ever let their voice be heard in a political meeting?

Intelligent reform of the law requires not only desire on the part of the reformer for a betterment of conditions, not only the political stamina and influence to get the legislative group to adopt his program, but most of all an intelligent understanding of legal history and precedent leading up to the existing dilemma, in order that the reformer will be able to point out to this age the factual errors of history. In drawing from the errors of the trial of Christ, therefore, a lesson in citizenship, it is well that we have in mind the history of law and the theory of human government. Archeology has its place in such a study but is quite beyond the scope of our brief presentation. The basic principles of the law have remained unchanged for four thousand years, and most of the great lawgivers of history have either been trained in the law or inspired of God. Somewhere the author has read that it was not mere accident that Moses was rescued from the river by Pharaoh's daughter, but that as a result of his upbringing in the royal palace Moses was educated in the Egyptian universities of that day and had some knowledge of existing law and of medicine as well. No doubt he had access to the Code of Hammurabi. Roman Law in force when Christ was tried, as we have pointed out, was the Laws of the Twelve Tables. Some years ago the author wrote his graduation thesis (unpublished) on "The Twelve Tables in Modern American Law" and demonstrated that 87 of the 113 sections of The Twelve Tables were in accord with our law, in principle if not in detail, in 1930 A.D., Two Thousand Three Hundred Eighty Years after they were promulgated! My brother has quite properly reminded the writer, time and time again, that the law is not an end unto itself but a means of enforcing some semblance of earthly justice until the world is raptured by the Second Coming of Christ: No man was ever saved by mere law!

The writings of St. Paul are very rich in their legal references. In our Appendix we mention the legalism of Paul in more detail. The Bible tells us he had been a student under the great and learned Gamaliel. Whether or not Paul was learned in the law, the idea of the Church as the Body of Christ is clearer to a legal mind if one remembers that corporations were known to law as far back as 500 B. C., and that corporate existence is the only worldly example of anything that resembles immortality.

Our point is that the legalisms in Paul's writings and the existence of corporations in those days in Greek and Roman Law—even the Hebrew corporate existence of the Sanhedrin—all aid one in understanding Christ. We will refer again to the precious promise that, "In My Father's house are many mansions, . . . I go to prepare a place for you." Archeology has discovered court records in Egypt in the Koine Greek language in which the word "Mansion" used in the passage quoted is used in the sense of "Habitable real estate acceptable for bail bond." We are sure our Heavenly Home will be habitable like that.

A great sage once said that one cannot stand still. The minute a movement stops growing, it deteriorates. As long as there were other worlds to conquer, Rome was a powerful state but when progress stopped the Empire fell. The public is prone to point out the laxities in our laws and government and lay the blame to two groups—the lawyers and the politicians. A failure of the Roman government to enforce the rigid laws in that great trial in Jerusalem caused the greatest public murder in history. From that failure we can learn the value of enforcement—the political lesson that the technicalities of a system of law should be enforced. We can learn that the remedy for a defective law is not wholesale violation but amendment.

So let us now as Christians use what influence we have to bring about those changes in Government and in law that will be for the greatest public good, remembering that good earthly government derives its power from the just consent of the governed. Let us teach the public to vote intelligently at every election, and to respect and obey the legal technicalities of existing government while working for their improvement. If we can thus educate the public to the intelligent use of elections we shall render real service to the people of the United States.

EPILOGUE—OUR REDEEMER

"Come unto me, all ye that labour and are heavy laden, and I will give you rest." Thus spoke Jesus of Nazareth, the Christ of God, the Saviour of the world—who in His earthly ministry never once used the word "religion." Christianity is not a religion; it is a revelation.

The word "religion" comes from a Greek root meaning the act of man searching out for God, pagan man trying to find God. But when Very God became flesh and dwelt among us, revealed Himself in the person of Christ, and died to save us from our sins, religion ceased for all believers in Jesus. True, many laymen and ministers use the term "Christian Religion" in a broad sense to embrace that which is actually Christian Revelation. We could quote columns of the words of The Master, and each would emphasize our point. During the trial before Pilate, Jesus made this startling statement: "Thou couldest have no power at all against me, except it were given thee from above." To a thief on a neighboring cross who confessed, He said: "Today shalt thou be with me in paradise." To His disciples; in that poignant fourteenth chapter of John, Jesus discussed the heavenly mansions He has gone to prepare for us, promised to return to take us there, and told us that the Father dwelleth in him to do the works.

Who could make these startling promises? Could an imposter make them and not be found out? What does the trial teach us of Our Redeemer? Did the Jews prove Jesus an imposter? If the trial proved Jesus was an imposter, why did Pilate have it inscribed on the cross, "THE KING OF THE JEWS" instead of, "He said he was king of the Jews."?

The reason is that the Jews failed to see the true import of the trial. This was not a trial of Christ by the Jews or by the Romans for that matter. It was a trial of the whole world by God Himself in the person of Christ, posing as a defendant, come to save the world, come in fulfillment of prophecy, come to die as the Lamb of God—the Paschal, sacrificial Lamb of God crucified to save men from their sins. The New Testament record constitutes not only an accurate fulfillment of prophecy, but its very words in some places quote the actual language of the great Jewish prophets. The crowd did spit in his face. He was crucified between two thieves and reviled by the crowd. The trial did follow the pattern of Isaiah 53. Jesus was trying the world. As the omnipotent Son of God, co-equal with God, Jesus knew everything. He knew the law. He had astonished the Rabbis with his legal knowledge when He was but twelve years old. He had power to make a legal record, to take an Appeal, to rely on the technicalities of the law, had He desired: but He knew He had to die to save the sinful world of men—and He went gloriously to his death saying, "Father, into Thy hands I commend my spirit."

No one can fully understand the technical legal violations of the Trial of Christ and not be impressed again with the accuracy in which God in His Grace has fulfilled such prophecies as that beautiful fifty-third chapter of Isaiah with which we close our study:

"1. Who hath believed our report? and to whom is the arm of the LORD revealed?

2. For he shall grow up before him as a tender plant, and as a root out of a dry ground: he hath no form nor comeliness; and when we shall see him, there is no beauty that we should desire him.

3. He is despised and rejected of men; a man of sorrows, and acquainted with grief: and we hid as it were our faces from him; he was despised, and we esteemed him not.

4. Surely he hath borne our griefs, and carried our sorrows: yet we did esteem him stricken, smitten of God, and afflicted.

5. But he was wounded for our transgressions, he was bruised for our iniquities: the chastisement of our peace was upon him; and with his stripes we are healed.

6. All we like sheep have gone astray; we have turned every one to his own way; and the LORD hath laid on him the iniquity of us all.

7. He was oppressed, and he was afflicted, yet he opened not his mouth: he is brought as a lamb to the slaughter, and as a sheep before her shearers is dumb, so he openeth not his mouth.

8. He was taken from prison and from judgment: and who shall declare his generation? for he was cut off out of the land of the living: for the transgression of my people was he stricken.

9. And he made his grave with the wicked, and with the rich in his death; because he had done no violence, neither was any deceit in his mouth.

10. Yet it pleased the LORD to bruise him; he hath put him to grief: when thou shalt make his soul an offering for sin, he shall see his seed, he shall prolong his days, and the pleasure of the LORD shall prosper in his hand.

11. He shall see of the travail of his soul, and shall be satisfied: by his knowledge shall my righteous servant justify many; for he shall bear their iniquities.

12. Therefore will I divide him a portion with the great, and he shall divide the spoil with the strong; because he hath poured out his soul unto death: and he was numbered with the transgressors; and he bare the sin of many, and made intercession for the transgressors."

APPENDIX A

LAWYERS IN THE SANHEDRIN

We have raised a question as to how far the Mosaic "lawyers" in the Sanhedrin were learned in secular law as we have used the term "law" in this work. The idea of St. Paul as a lawyer, for example, is referred to in passing in Smith, Life and Letters of St. Paul, p. 30; Xenophan P. Wilfley, St. Paul the Herald of Christianity, pp. 17 & 22; Encyclopedia of Religion & Ethics, XI, p. 185; Goldberg & Benderly, Outline of Jewish Knowledge, Student's Edition, III, p. 516; Edersheim, op. cit., II 556; Wigmore's Panorama of the World's Legal Systems (1 vol. "Desk" reprint 1928) pp. 113 and 119 quoting Mischna, V, on Sanhedrin application of the civil law of bailments; Whiston's edition of Josephus' Works, p. 497; Peloubet's Bible Dictionary, p. 591. None of these except Senator Wilfley refers to Paul as a lawyer but we know that Paul was a Pharisee, and a member of the Sanhedrin, and that the Sanhedrin had legislative, executive, judicial, civil, criminal and ecclesiastical power under the Romans, only Roman Citizens having a right of appeal to Rome. Paul's writings abound in references to Roman Law which, judging from their content, he must have known considerable about; see Acts 25:8; Gal. 3:15; I Tim., Chap. 1; and Wilfley, op. cit.

According to a concordance at hand, the word "Lawyer" is found in the Bible only in the following usages:

(1) Matt. 22:35: "then one of them, which was a lawyer, asked him a question, tempting him, and saying," (Great Commandment).

(2) Luke 7:30: "But the Pharisees and lawyers rejected the counsel of God—."

(3) Luke 10:25: "And, behold, a certain lawyer stood up, and tempted him, saying . . ."

(4) Luke 11:45 ff: Several references where Jesus rebuked the Pharisees and Lawyers for too much ritualism and (v. 52) for throwing away the key of knowledge. Did he mean that they were trying to make legal exactitude a substitute for salvation? This passage may be basis for our very argument that as Christians we should observe but alter harsh technicalities of law!

(5) Luke 14:3: "And Jesus answering spake unto the lawyers and Pharisees—"concerning eating meat on the sabbath and also teaching that Acts of Mercy are always permissible.

(6) Titus 3:13: "Bring Zenas the lawyer and Apollos on their journey diligently—."

In Luke, the closing part of the second chapter, we find a narrative of Jesus staying behind at the age of twelve, discussing with the Doctors in the Temple and amazing them with his knowledge, but the record does not show any legal discussions.

For our own part, we cannot see how the Sanhedrists could handle civil and criminal matters unless they knew civil and criminal law. Mr. Wilfley, an astute exemplar at the Bar in St. Louis for half a century before his death about 1940, is the only modern lawyer whom we have found writing a life of Paul, and we feel satisfied to hold with him that the Sanhedrists and Paul were trained in secular law. We agree that they were primarily church luminaries, dealing with and interpreting the Mosaic Law, but when we consider that seven of the ten commandments and much of the other Mosaic Law is enforced in our courts today, and that Paul quoted Roman Law with unfailing accuracy, the conclusion seems to us unescapable that the Sanhedrists were learned in the law, even though not practicing lawyers in a modern sense. We regret that limitations of space and scope of this brief study prevent further discussion of this interesting issue. It is significant that in his "Trial of Christ", Rabbi Drucker tries to repudiate Christ by showing that the Sanhedrists were too good lawyers to be a party to such a farcical "trial."

APPENDIX B

BIBLIOGRAPHY

The following authorities have been cited or referred to in this work: (Listed in the Order of Citation) *

The Holy Bible

Edward J. White, Esq., The Law in the Scriptures, (Thomas Law Book Company, St. Louis).

Sir William Blackstone, Esq., Commentaries on the Laws of England, (1765) Cooley's 2nd Amer. Edn. (1876).

Rev. Clarence Edward Macartney, Trials of Great Men of the Bible.

Rev. Harry Rimmer, Voices from the Silent Centuries.

Rev. William F. Albright, From the Stone Age to Christianity.

Prof. John H. Wigmore, Esq., A Panorama of the World's Legal Systems.

Rev. Alfred Edersheim, The Life and Times of Jesus The Messiah.

Thayer's, Greek-English Lexicon.

Corpus Juris, (a 72 volume modern legal encyclopedia not to be confused with the Justinian Corpus Juris Civilis also referred to).

Missouri Code of Civil Procedure (1945) passed in 1943 and effective January 1, 1945; Laws Mo., '43, p. 389.

James M. Rollins, Esq., The Arrest, Trial and Conviction of Jesus Christ from a Lawyer's Standpoint.

Rabbi A. P. Drucker, The Trial of Jesus from Jewish Sources.

W. M. Chandler, Esq., The Trial of Jesus from a Lawyer's Standpoint.

Mischna. Pirke Aboth.

Rev. R. H. Strachan, The Fourth Gospel.

Josephus, Antiquities.

Emmanuel Deutsch, The Talmud.

U. S. Constitution, Amendments V & VI & XIV.

The Trial of Christ 49

Missouri Constitution, (1875) Art. II Sec. 23; (1945) Art. I, Sec. 19.

The Twelve Tables (450 B. C.) Conant's Translation in St. Louis Law Review, June, 1928 (Bruns' Text).

Court opinion, Jacobs v. Danciger, 328 Mo. 458.

Rabbi Mendelsohn, Criminal Jurisprudence of the Ancient Hebrews.

Rabbi Joseph Klausner, Jesus of Nazareth.

Peloubet's Bible Dictionary

Tacitus, Annals.

Court Opinion, Rose v. Knobeloch, 194 S. W. 2d, 943.

Court Opinions, Hauptmann v. State, 116 N. J. L. 412 and other books (Lindbergh Kidnapping Case).

Whiston, Editor, Works of Josephus.

Rev. David Smith, The Life and Letters of St. Paul.

Xenophon P. Wilfley, Esq., St. Paul the Herald of Christianity.

Encyclopedia of Religion and Ethics.

Profs. Goldberg & Benderly, Student's Outline of Jewish Knowledge.

Judicial Code of The United States, in various law books.

Prof. John H. Wigmore, Esq., Law of Evidence.

Court Opinion, State v. Faber, (Mo. 1945) 182 S. W. 2d 552.

Revised Statutes of Missouri, 1939, Sec. 907.

Missouri Constitution of 1945, Art. I Sec. 18.

Bouvier's Law Dictionary.

Court Opinion, Bailey v. Drexel Furniture Co., 259 U. S. 20.

Rev. H. Framer Smith, "The Romance of the Greek New Testament" in The Sunday School Times, Feb. 1, 1947.

Gaius' Institutes.

McCune Gill, Esq., "Getting Back to Justinian", in American Law Review, vol. 62 p. 301; (1928).

Sir John Legge, Esq., Confucian Analects. Prof. Rudolph Sohm, Institutes of Roman Law, (Ledlie's Translation, Oxford, 1926).

Sir Henry S. Maine, Esq., Ancient Laws.

Ulpian, Frag.

Court Opinion, Dartmouth College v. Woodward, 4 Wheaton 518.

Court Opinion, Hudson Bay Co.'s Governors v. Hudson Bay Fur Co., 33 Fed. 2d 801.

Rev. Ernest Gordon, "A Survey of Religious Life and Thought", in The Sunday School Times, January 11, 1947.

www.ingramcontent.com/pod-product-compliance
Lightning Source LLC
Chambersburg PA
CBHW031436040426
42444CB00006B/834